Slide and Slurp, Scratch and Burp

More about Verbs

To Isabella
—B.P.C.

Verb: A word that shows action or being

Slide and Slurp, Scratch and Burp

More about Verbs

by Brian P. Cleary

illustrated by Brian Gable

SCHOLASTIC INC.
New York Toronto London Auckland Sydney
Mexico City New Delhi Hong Kong Buenos Aires

Verbs are words like sneak and sniff,

sneeze and seize

and wheeze and whiff.

Planting carrots,
getting traction,
Verbs give sentences
their action.

You might be exploring
the Alps or the Amazon,
maybe restoring
the chair that your grandma's on.

knitting or hitting
or roping or biting—
verbs can make sentences
very exciting.

They tell us of horses

that nuzzle and nip,

of bears as
they guzzle

and birds as they sip.

They tell us of scooters both swerving and stopping,

throws that are curving or sliding or dropping.

9

So wrap a package, tie a knot,

clap your hands, or cry a lot.

Triumph, tremble,

trot, and trample,

you'll use a **Verb**
for each example!

Fly to the flower shop,
dash to the dance,

swing by the swimming pool,

frolic in France.

Soar to the circus and float to the fair.

Without verbs, your sentence can't go anywhere.

Each sentence **has** a subject—
it's kind of like the star.

It's what the whole thing's all about:

Dave's dish,

Mom's look,

Todd's car.

Subjects always need a verb—
it's what makes fishes swim

and lanterns light
and writers write
and clippers cut and trim.

Some **Verbs** aren't the action kind—
They "**link**" instead of "**do**,"

connecting sentence parts, as in,
"Your dog appears quite blue."

These linking verbs connect a subject to a word or phrase

that's called a subject complement. It's done in lots of ways:

It became ridiculous.

That strudel sure smells great.

The crime remains a mystery.

This play seems second rate.

21

The forms of "be"
are linking verbs,

like, "Are your names Michelle?"

Were and was
work this way, too—
they're forms of "be" as well.

I am Shannon.
He is Mort.

Were you the one
who was in court?

There **are** times
a form of "be"
is all that's **needed**, verbally.

Whether you slide

or you slip

or you slurp,

if you should scream

or you scratch

or you burp,

if you're making a fraction
or writing a blurb,

because there is action,
you know it's a verb.

So if you should gloat

or you glisten

or listen,

say to the chef, "Take that out and put this in."

Whether you pounce

or pronounce

or perturb,

I'm here to announce
that you're using a verb!

So, what is a verb?

Do you know?

ABOUT THE AUTHOR & ILLUSTRATOR

BRIAN P. CLEARY is the author of the Words Are Categorical™ and Math Is Categorical™ series, as well as Rainbow Soup: Adventures in Poetry and Rhyme and PUNishment: Adventures in Wordplay. He lives in Cleveland, Ohio.

BRIAN GABLE is the illustrator of many Words Are Categorical™ books, the Math Is Categorical™ series, and the Make Me Laugh! joke books. He lives in Toronto, Ontario, with his wife and two children.

ISBN-13: 978-0-545-04755-5
ISBN-10: 0-545-04755-2

12 11 10 9 8 7 6 5 4 3 2 1   8 9 10 11 12 13/0

Printed in the U.S.A.   23

First Scholastic printing, January 2008